The American Swedish Institute

A Living Heritage

Sherry Butcher-Younghans

American Swedish Institute

KENDALL/HUNT PUBLISHING COMPANY
2460 Kerper Boulevard P.O. Box 539 Dubuque, Iowa 52004-0539

Contents

Preface

It is a pleasure and a distinct honor for me to write a preface to this beautiful volume. For almost half a century I have been associated with the American Swedish Institute in one way or another—first as a member going back to the early 1940's, contributing occasionally to its first publication, *The Bulletin,* secondly serving as its Director from 1967 to 1973, and of late as a distant member viewing its progress and development into one of the finest cultural institutions in the Upper Northwest.

During its close to six decades of existence the Institute has constantly and consistently endeavored to carry out the program and ideas of its donor, Swan Johan Turnblad, in presenting to Americans of Swedish descent the very finest of Swedish arts, literature and science.

It is therefore a fitting tribute to the memory of its founder and principal donor that Mrs. Sherry Butcher-Younghans has compiled this descriptive volume concerned with the magnificent structure on Park Avenue in Minneapolis. In doing this she has dwelled on its history, its architecture, its collections and finally has given us a look at what the Institute's aims and goals are, its programs and cultural activities.

The visitor who enters the galleries of the American Swedish Institute, with this guide to its many treasures, will come away with a better understanding and appreciation of what the preservation of the Swedish cultural heritage means.

Nils William Olsson

Acknowledgments

I wish to gratefully acknowledge Wendy R. Egan and Richard W. Helgerson for reading and editing the manuscript at every stage and offering their insightful comments and helpful suggestions.

Also, I wish to thank my research associate, Lawrence Hammerstrom, whose intuition and accumulated knowledge about the Turnblad family have been an invaluable resource in the writing of this book.

To the readers of the manuscript: Fred G. Anderson, Marvin Anderson, Timothy Blade, Lawrence Hammerstrom, Mary Mueller, Byron Nordstrom, Beverly Norris, Christopher Olsson, Emil Ostrom and Mary Swanson, I give my most sincere thanks for their careful review and wise suggestions.

Several specialists contributed their valuable time and expertise in the compiling of information necessary for this book; I thank Marvin Anderson, Andrea Blum, Dee Buelow, Susan Larson-Fleming, Alan Lathrop, Peter Kessler, and Curt Pederson.

The process of gathering information was facilitated with the assistance of the Albin Polasek Foundation, the Minneapolis History Collection, the Minneapolis Public Library and the Northwest Architectural Archives.

Many of the historic photographs for the book were selected from the American Swedish Institute Archives with the assistance of Marita Karlisch and Jeannette Helgerson. Other photographs were taken by Jerry Taube, Mel Jacobson, Harland Nasvik, and Bernice Wenzel.

And, finally, my deepest thanks to my husband, Tom, and my sons Nicholas and Neal, who are invariably patient and encouraging.

The American Swedish Institute.

Introduction

The founder of the American Swedish Institute was a dreamer.

The record of his life—what little we have of it—shows him as a capable and hard-working publisher; an astute and successful businessman.

In those qualities he was not unique. What made him different was his vision, a vision he first glimpsed more than 80 years ago, when he began to plan for the castle-like mansion that stands at 2600 Park Avenue in Minneapolis.

He built his home on the grand scale of other mansions of that time and place, but as the years went by, he saw the magnificent building as a place where the Swedish heritage and culture could be nurtured and preserved.

He dreamed and built better than he knew.

Today, the mansion built by Swan Johan Turnblad shelters the American Swedish Institute. It stands, not as a sterile monument to the past, but as a living and dynamic center for the preservation of the American-Swedish culture and all of the activities that purpose implies.

Some 40,000 persons come through its doors every year; more than 7,000 claim membership in the Institute.

Some see the Institute almost as a second home, a warm and welcoming place where they meet their friends and speak their native tongue.

Others come because the Institute houses the numerous Swedish-American organizations to which they belong, and which offer links to the past and the heritage they cherish.

Still others visit the Institute as they would visit any other museum; to see the architecture, richly carved interiors, and the thousands of artifacts from the emigration period.

Visitors can see Swedish art, trace their Swedish roots, learn Swedish handcrafts, dances, or language, or as often as not, simply absorb some of the spirit of the Swedish-American experience.

Whatever their reasons, it is the presence of the members and visitors, and their participation, that gives life to the Institute.

Swan Turnblad's dream has come true. The home he built with such pride has become the place where the Swedish-American culture lives today and will live for generations to come.

I. Swan Johan Turnblad

Portrait of ASI founder, Swan Johan Turnblad, by Christian von Schneidau.

During the early 20th century, Swan Johan Turnblad was hailed as one of the most successful Swedes in the U.S., and the foremost of Swedish newspapermen in America.[1] He built one of the largest Swedish language newspapers in the country, amassing a substantial fortune in the process. Along with this prosperity came social prominence and civic involvement. Before his death, Turnblad was seen as a visionary and philanthropist who made a significant impact on the history and development of Minnesota.

Swan Johan Turnblad was born Sven Johan Månsson, a name that was changed when he immigrated. His life began much the same as others who left their native country for the promising "New Land." Turnblad was born on October 7, 1860 into a poor farming family that owned a small tract of land in Tubbemåla, Småland, Sweden. In 1868, at the age of eight, Turnblad, along with his parents, Olof and Ingrid, and three siblings, left famine-stricken Sweden. His family had sold their farm to purchase passage on the ship *S. S. City of New York.*

Olof and Ingrid Månsson, from Vasa Illustrata *written by Eric Norelius.*

The Månsson family farmstead located in Långhult Norregård, Ryssby, Kronoberg Län, Småland, Sweden.

The Early Years

After the Turnblads arrived in New York they traveled to Minnesota where they settled in the Swedish community of Vasa in Goodhue County, joining relatives who had come earlier. It was a common practice for Swedish immigrants to settle in communities that were reconstructed in much the same way as those that they had left behind, often having even the same neighbors as they had in Sweden.

Turnblad lived in Vasa for ten years, until he was eighteen. During this time the Turnblad family farmed the land that they had settled, while Swan pursued his interest in printing. It was in Vasa that he is said to have printed an arithmetic book for the schoolmaster, P. T. Lindholm. Oral history suggests that the printing of the book took young Turnblad six months and each of the book's 129 pages was set by hand.[2] (A copy of this book, *Praktisk Lärobok i Aritmetik,* is in the ASI Archives.)

In 1879 Turnblad traveled to Minneapolis to learn the printing trade. He worked as a typesetter for several Swedish language newspapers including *Minnesota Stats Tidning* (1881–1883) and *Svenska Folkets Tidning* (1883–1886). In 1887 Turnblad was listed in the *Minneapolis Directory* as the "manager" of the Swedish-American newspaper called *Svenska Amerikanska Posten.* It was this publication that he eventually came to own. Turnblad's fortune was founded on its remarkable success.

Svenska Amerikanska Posten

The first issue of the *Svenska Amerikanska Posten* was published on March 10, 1885. The newspaper's first publisher was Nils Peter Lind, who published the weekly to promote temperance principles and social reform. Lind's zealous nature and intolerant attitudes alienated many potential subscribers, with the

Swan J. Turnblad.

result that there was little interest in subscribing to, or advertising in, the controversial paper.

When Turnblad was hired as the *Svenska Amerikanska Posten* manager less than two years after its inception, he recognized the inherent problems in the paper's management. He undertook to change this by broadening the paper's views, taking a more liberal, non-religious and socially progressive approach.

After Turnblad became manager, circulation began to soar. By the early 20th century the weekly paper had a circulation of more than 40,000, up substantially from the 1400 subscribers it claimed in its first two years.

A page from the July 21, 1903 issue of Svenska Amerikanska Posten.

late 19th and early 20th centuries. These incoming, first-generation immigrants were dependent upon the Swedish language newspapers as a means of understanding their new culture. The *Svenska Amerikanska Posten,* with its news from "back home," around the world and locally, made the publication a valuable resource for the immigrant. It also served as a cohesive force for Swedish-Americans and assisted in perpetuating their ethnicity. Turnblad was aware of the impact his newspaper made on this ethnic group and took advantage of the times. Under Turnblad's direction the paper became "an influence that did much to shape conditions, ever laboring for what was elevating and tended to better citizenship."[3]

Much of the success of the *Svenska Amerikanska Posten* resulted not only from its popular and useful contents but came from Turnblad's aggressive management style and business acumen. He wanted to create a technically advanced newspaper, and to achieve this he purchased the best printing equipment available. He became the first Swedish publisher in America to set his paper by a Linotype machine and he later bought a Mergenthaler press. In 1903 he became the first Swedish-American publisher to own a duplex rotary color printing press, enabling him to create color illustrations.[4]

Another innovation that Turnblad offered his subscribers was the use of a public reading room with Swedish and American newspapers and a lending library. Turnblad purchased a large number of books from J. B. Gans' library in Gothenburg, Sweden for his lending library. Subscribers were encouraged to use the library that was installed in the building that housed the newspaper. Many of these volumes are now a part of the library and archives' collections at the American Swedish Institute.

Turnblad became the owner of the *Svenska Amerikanska Posten* by October 1897, controlling more than 95% of the corporation's shares. Under Turnblad's direction the publication had become, as he advertised it, the "Biggest! Best! Cheapest! America's Leading Swedish-language Newspaper."

A major factor in the paper's success was the influx of Swedish immigrants during the

In 1915, assured of a prosperous future for the *Svenska Amerikanska Posten* newspaper, Swan Turnblad erected a three story building to house his business, simply called the "Posten Building."

The *Svenska Amerikanska Posten* continued to be a successful ethnic newspaper until 1920 when it was sold to Magnus Martinson. Swan Turnblad was approaching his sixtieth birthday and had made a fortune from his publication. For more than thirty years he had served as publisher and at times editor of the paper. It is believed that Turnblad had grown tired of publishing and wanted instead to devote his time to public affairs.

The buyer, Magnus Martinson, a former Lutheran minister, was himself a Swedish immigrant who had some previous experience in newspaper management. Martinson continued the publication of the *Svenska Amerikanska Posten* until 1927 when the paper became insolvent and a local bank took it over, at which time Turnblad was called back to resurrect the business. He paid off the debts and resumed his position as sole owner in 1928. It was only a year later that Turnblad donated his newspaper, along with the Posten Building and his palatial estate, to the newly-formed American Institute for Swedish Arts, Literature, and Science. Turnblad continued as publisher until his death in 1933, when his only child, Lillian, became publisher. Publication of the ethnic newspaper continued until September 11, 1940, after the Institute's Board of Trustees had sold the newspaper's subscription list to *Svenska Amerikanaren Tribunen* in Chicago on August 23, 1940. In 1954, the museum's board sold the Posten Building to the Hudson Products Company. The building was demolished in December 1983, with only a stained glass window being saved and restored. In 1986, this window was installed in the American Swedish Institute Museum, as a remembrance of Turnblad's newspaper enterprise.

Turnblad at his desk in the Posten building located at 500 S. 7th Street.

Publisher Magnus Martinson and his secretary, Hannah Swanson, in his office in the Posten Building, circa 1920s.

Turnblad's Financial Growth

As Swan Turnblad's newspaper business expanded so did his other financial investments. He invested in real estate and between the years of 1882 and 1915 purchased several Minnesota properties. In 1882 he and his brother-in-law, Charles Fridlund, purchased a single family house at 2007 South 4th Street in Minneapolis. In 1892 Turnblad bought property at 1511 Stevens Avenue and built a three-story apartment that was called Cecil Flats. Turnblad and his family lived at this residence until he built the mansion at 2600 Park Avenue in Minneapolis. In 1899 he purchased a lot on Oak Grove Street in Loring Park, where he wanted to build an opulent residence. This lot was the last one remaining in the Loring Park system. In 1901, the Board of Park Commissioners condemned the property for park purposes and Turnblad was forced to relinquish the land in 1902.

After having to abandon his original plan, Turnblad purchased property at 2600 Park Avenue in Minneapolis in the following year. In 1904 blueprints were drawn and construction was begun on his house.

Exterior view of Turnblad's apartment building, Cecil Flats.

The Turnblad residence, located on the first floor of the Cecil Flats apartment building. Taken by Dempsie Photography in Minneapolis.

In 1908, Turnblad sold his Cecil Flats apartment building and moved into his Park Avenue mansion.

At about the same time he purchased 4,332 acres of land in Pine County, Minnesota, which he hoped to develop into a Swedish farming community. On May 4, 1909 he advertised the availability of the agricultural land in the *Svenska Amerikanska Posten*. Here he called it "Ny Svensk Koloni i Minnesota" (a New Swedish Colony in Minnesota.) Turnblad encouraged his readers to inquire about the property by extolling its agricultural potential. His dreams for this Swedish farming colony never materialized.

Family Life
It was through the temperance movement that Swan Turnblad met his wife. In the early 1880s a temperance organization, known as

The Turnblad family, circa 1892, taken at J. A. Brush Studio in Minneapolis.

Lillian Turnblad, circa 1885.

Freya Society, was established and meetings were held on Washington Avenue, in the Seven Corners area in Minneapolis. Turnblad was a faithful member of this organization, and there he met Christina (Nilsson) Nelson. She, like Turnblad, was Swedish, and had emigrated with her family from the province of Jämtland, Sweden.

Christina had come to Worthington, Minnesota, in 1876 when she was 15 years old. Her first job gave her experience and English language training, but she earned no wages. Later she was employed as a "dining room" girl for one year during which time she earned $153.53. In 1882, when Christina was 21, she came to Minneapolis where she met the young newspaper manager. They were married in 1883, and a year later the Turnblad's only child, Lillian Zenobia, was born.

Civic Involvement

Swan Turnblad was active in many civic affairs and by the turn of the century had become an affluent member of Minneapolis society. Although he never ran for public office, Turnblad held a number of leadership positions in the community. He organized the first Swedish lodge of Good Templars in Minnesota. Turnblad was a 32nd degree Freemason, of the Ancient Arabic Order, Nobles of the Mystic Shrine. He was a member of the Fraternal Order of Elks, as well as a member of the Minneapolis Athletic Club, Automobile Club, and the Minneapolis Civic and Commerce Association. He was a charter member of a Scandinavian-American social organization called the Odin Club. Turnblad served as a member of the Memorial Commission for the Swedish inventor John Ericsson.

Turnblad's influence was not restricted to fraternal and social organizations; he also was involved in Minnesota's political affairs. He served as a delegate to Democratic national conventions, in 1904 and 1908. In 1899 Governor Lind appointed him a member of the Board of Managers of the state reformatory at St. Cloud, a post he held until 1901. Although they were never close friends, Turnblad supported Lind and used his paper to convey their similar political views. John Lind and Turnblad were both immigrants from Småland, Sweden. Their families emigrated in the same year, 1868, and both families settled in Vasa, Minnesota.

Turnblad was appointed to the State Board of Visitors for Public Institutions by Governor John A. Johnson and was retained through three administrations (1907–1921). In 1905 he was commissioned as Colonel of the Minnesota National Guard for Governor Johnson. He served in this position until 1917.

Turnblad's influence and assistance reached back to his mother country as well. In 1926, Swedish King Gustav V conferred upon Turnblad the medal of the Order of the North Star. This was bestowed upon him for his humanitarian contribution of $20,000, which he raised through his newspaper, for the relief of the people in northern Sweden who suffered from a serious crop failure in 1902.

Swan Turnblad dressed in the uniform of the Minnesota National Guard. He served as Colonel from 1905 until 1917 for four Governors.

From The Minneapolis Journal, *September 28, 1908, with the caption "Democratic Leader and Minneapolis Friends at Ex-Governor John Lind's Home." First row: S. M. Owen, John Lind, W. J. Bryan, and Fred B. Lynch.*

Back row: Swan J. Turnblad, M. C. Brady, Julius V. Heinrich, Dr. K. Hoegh, F. C. McMillan, Judge F. C. Brooks, Frank Larrabee, Judge Fred V. Brown, W. M. Jerome, and Mayor James C. Haynes.

Turnblad's Horseless Carriage

It was typical of Turnblad to be the first to own a commercially made automobile in Minneapolis. This conspicuous ownership attracted attention in the city when he operated the car for the first time in the spring of 1900.

On Tuesday, April 10, 1900, *The Minneapolis Journal* reported:

"The first private electric automobile appeared on the streets last evening. It belongs to Swan J. Turnblad, proprietor of the Svenska Amerikanska Posten, *and created somewhat of a sensation as it rolled along Nicollet Avenue carrying the owner and a party of friends.*

"The vehicle is one of the latest patterns with all the latest improvements. It will run from thirty to forty miles without being recharged and it can be regulated to five different degrees of speed. Mr. Turnblad has placed a small electric plant in his barn with which he recharges the carriage whenever necessary."[5]

Somewhat later, Turnblad became incensed at an article in *The Minneapolis Journal* entitled "They Get Habits On," in which the writer called attention to the unreliability of automobiles. Turnblad wrote a lengthy and spirited reply, which was printed on July 25, 1900, saying:

"In your Saturday issue I noticed an article headed "They Get Habits On" in regard to automobiles, saying that breakdowns of autos have occurred so often that the confidence of auto owners is shaken, etc.

"I believe I was the first owner of an auto (electric) in this city having one of the Waverly Dos-a-Dos since last Spring. So far I have never had a hitch or breakdown having used my vehicle more or less every day or evening since I got it, running from five to thirty-five miles each trip, making hills and grades in the vicinity of Minneapolis with four of us in it, and I believe you do an injustice and misrepresent the autos in your article.

"A breakdown may and will happen to any vehicle sometimes but I feel just as safe returning home in my electric auto as I would with a pair of lovely horses.

Turnblad in his electric Waverly, the first commercially-built automobile in Minneapolis.

"The electric auto has several advantages over a rig drawn by horses. First, it is always ready; secondly, it never gets tired out, that is, until the charge is consumed and with my auto I can travel on a level roadbed sixty miles, but on ups and downs, as we have them here around Minneapolis, probably only fifty miles without recharging. The third reason why I value my auto ahead of a rig drawn by horses is the fact that it is clean and breezy, kicking up no dirt or dust, giving the full benefits of the bracing air, especially so in hot weather, when horses will sweat and when dusty or muddy, they will kick up the dust and dirt.

Swan, Christina and Lillian Turnblad in front of Cecil Flats apartment.

"I have no experience with steam or gasoline autos but believe that if they are properly understood and taken care of they will prove satisfactory, but I am sure that any electric rig, if they act and serve well as mine has done so far, will be placed ahead of a horse rig. I would not trade my electric auto, providing I could not buy another one, for any span of horses and Victoria in Minneapolis even if it included a coachman's services free of charge for one year, and would not sell my electric auto at any price if I could not buy another one.

"I have heard the remark it is not enough of a sport to ride in an auto. Well, try going at a speed of twenty-two or twenty-three miles an hour and I believe such parties will find it sport enough. I can get home from Lake Harriet to 1511 Stevens Avenue in less than fif-teen minutes and without my auto-horse sweaty or tired out, run the rig into the barn, put the charging plug into same and in a few minutes it is again ready for fifty or sixty miles run.

"Another reason why I prefer an auto instead of a horse rig is that it is less expensive, costing only about one-half cents per running mile, and it does not eat oats when not used. I have so far not spent a dollar on repairs or wear and tear, used very little oil and grease as everything is fitted with ball bearings.

"I am no agent for any company, and the above is written wholly to protest against the injustice done the autos as a whole and mine in particular, in the article above referred to does not make any exceptions.

—Swan J. Turnblad[6]

Interior of the Turnblad's Cecil Flats apartment.

Life in the Mansion

A question frequently asked by visitors to the museum is: "Did the Turnblads ever really live in the house?" Since so much history concerning the Turnblads is steeped in myth and misinformation this question is not easily answered.

The Turnblads were a reserved family and kept very much to themselves. Little is known about the family's personal life and few records were kept. It is only through historical sources found in the ASI archives, transcribed oral histories and personal communications with friends, distant relatives, and former employees, that the Turnblads' life and habits have been partially reconstructed.

Evidence indicates that the Turnblad family lived in the mansion from approximately 1908 until 1915 when they moved into their newly constructed Posten Building. Support for this view comes from a document written by Swedish Vice Consul, Nils Jaenson, in 1929 in which he says that the Turnblads lived in the newspaper building where "an elegant apartment is installed."[7] A former newspaper employee, Hilda Benson, supports this in her memoirs, affirming that the family spent their nights on the Posten Building's third floor.[8]

Before 1908 the family lived in the apartment building called Cecil Flats that was owned by Turnblad. It is reasonable to assume that the Turnblads moved into the Park Avenue estate in 1908 because records show that the plumbing was completed during this year. The *Minneapolis Directory* lists the Turnblads as residing at 2600 Park Avenue from 1905, but this is unlikely because the house would have been under construction at this time.

It is clear that the mansion was vacant for a number of years before it was converted into

Exterior of the former Turnblad mansion, circa 1930s.

a museum. A newspaper article from the *Minneapolis Tribune* dated March 9, 1921, revealed that the estate was broken into by four youths who noticed the house was always empty and they wondered if it might be haunted. The boys trespassed to see if they could find any ''ghosts around the place.''9 Turnblad was not amused and charged the boys with trespassing. Each was fined five dollars for his inquisitiveness about the supernatural. (This was later changed by the judge to two dollars.)

The Turnblads probably lived in the Posten Building until it was donated to the American Institute for Swedish Arts, Literature, and Science in 1929, along with the Park Avenue estate. It was reported by Nils Jaenson that Swan Turnblad and daughter Lillian (Christina, Swan's wife, had died on September 6, 1929) lived in an unidentified Minneapolis hotel from 1929 until 1930. In 1930 they moved into two rented apartments located at 2615 Park Avenue, across the street from the American Swedish Institute. Swan Turnblad lived at this location until his death on May 17, 1933. After her father's death, Lillian moved to The Academy of the Holy Angels in Minneapolis. She died on October 19, 1943.

From Mansion to Museum

On December 9, 1929, Swan Turnblad publicly announced his decision to establish his mansion as the American Institute for Swedish Arts, Literature, and Science. (In 1949 the name was changed to the American Swedish Institute.) The gift, as previously noted, included the Posten Building and the *Svenska Amerikanska Posten* newspaper. Swan Turnblad along with his daughter Lillian, jointly dedicated the gift. Turnblad's wife, Christina had died in September of that year and her interest in the property was included in the contribution. (In February 1929, all three members of the family signed a document in which they agreed to donate their mansion as an institute but this was not acted upon until December of that year.)

Headlines of several Minneapolis newspapers announced the gift: "Turnblad Says Home Built For Museum Use," "Reveals Dream Nurtured For 25 Years Near Fulfillment," "Publisher Seeking Closer Link Between Native and Adopted Lands," "Home Given as Swedish Art Museum." Turnblad publicly stated that he had long intended for his estate to be a Swedish-American institute, and now his dream was being fulfilled. He further said that, "many persons may have wondered what a small family like ours, a family which had not great social ambitions wanted with so big a house. Perhaps they can guess now."[10]

It is doubtful that Turnblad built the mansion for the sole purpose of using it as a museum. It is more likely that factors such as Turnblad's age (69), the fifteen-year vacancy of the property, and possibly the high property taxes influenced his decision. Other possible ways of disposing of the building were explored by Turnblad before he made his decision to convert his home. Included in these options was the possibility of giving the property to the Swedish state as a consulate building, or making it a permanent location for the Odin Club, an existing Scandinavian organization.

Whatever Turnblad's reasons for founding the American Swedish Institute, it is clear that he wanted to preserve and perpetuate the Swedish heritage in Minnesota. He strongly believed in education and saw his museum as a way to reach the public with his cause.

Turnblad said about his institute that "it will be first of all American." "I am American. There is nobody more loyal to this country than I am; and I stand ready to shoulder a gun in proof of that loyalty if it ever should be necessary. But I am also a native of Sweden, and I hold dear many things which are Swedish. It has seemed to me to be desirable for both countries if some of the products of Swedish culture might be shown here."[11]

The new museum established by Turnblad was a remarkable structure, unlike any other in the area. It featured a hand-carved two-story fireplace, extensively carved dining room and music room and a library with thousands of volumes. From his own collection he donated paintings, etchings, sculpture, porcelain urns, handwoven rugs and stained glass windows. In addition, his gift included an incomparable collection of Swedish porcelain tile stoves. The combined value of the Turnblad estate and the Posten Building was publicized as being worth one and a half million dollars.[12]

The Museum: Its Beginnings

From 1929 to 1932 the attendance at Turnblad's institute was a disappointment. Because of its limited hours and scanty publicity, few people came to the newly established "American Institute for Swedish Arts, Literature, and Science," as it was first called. But with Turnblad's usual persistence and with his interest in education he appointed several Swedish-American scholars to organize special exhibits, programs and lectures for a public opening of the museum.[13]

Thus in 1933 the mansion was reopened as a museum with exhibits of Swedish artifacts—both old and new. As an adjunct to the newly installed exhibits, many educational and cultural programs were offered. The exhibits were displayed on all three floors of the museum, making for a spectacular attraction. It was reported that in the 10 day opening of "Cultural Week" more than 20,000 visitors appeared to view the museum.[14] The American Swedish Institute was finally off to a strong start and has from that time been supported by the Swedish-American community and the community at large. It has attracted a large membership, exceeding 7,000 today.

The American Institute for Swedish Arts, Literature, and Science, as it was called until 1949, when it was re-named the American Swedish Institute.

Aerial view of the ASI.

II. From the Ground Up: 2600 Park Avenue

In 1903 Swan Johan Turnblad purchased six city lots between Oakland Avenue and Park Avenue in Minneapolis from the George F. Roberts family. The affluent sought to build their showpiece homes in this neighborhood. In 1889 a publication by the Minneapolis Board of Trade stated that "Park Avenue is noted for the many beautiful homes that adorn it and ranks as the finest residence street in the city."[15]

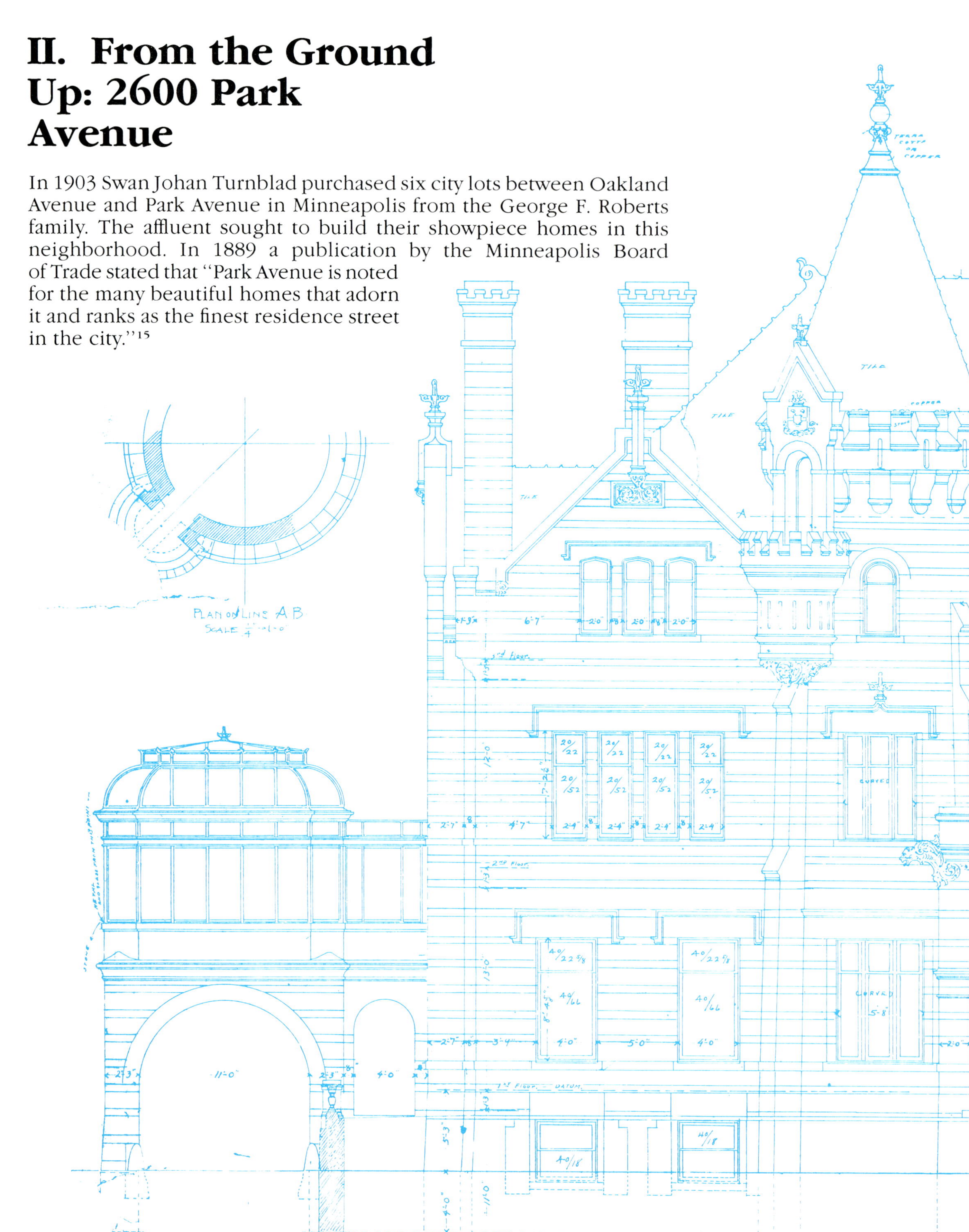

Blueprint of the Turnblad mansion, by architects Christopher A. Boehme and Victor Cordella, which was drawn up in 1904.

Chateauesque features of the mansion include the circular turrets and steep conical roofs. Turnblad's initials and the date, 1904, are carved into the limestone.

At the turn of the century it was common practise to display one's accumulated wealth by building grandiose estates. It was on Park Avenue that Turnblad chose to build his mansion, near the estates of other leading citizens of Minneapolis, including the Pillsburys, McKnights, Peaveys, Bells, Sawyers and Phelps.

After securing the lots on Park Avenue, Turnblad went about finding an architectural firm that would design a home beyond compare. Architectural designs were submitted by, W. H. Dennis of Minneapolis, Frank G. Cauffman of Pennsylvania, and Boehme and Cordella of Minneapolis. Turnblad opted for the elaborate and ornamental chateau style presented by Christopher A. Boehme (1865–1916) and Victor Cordella (1872–1937). The blueprints were drawn in 1904 and construction on the mansion began in that year.

The mansion that was built on the site has been described as a Swedish castle or a grown-up's doll house. It is a "Chateauesque" design that was derived from a 16th century French style, also known as Francis I. Features of "Chateauesque" architecture can be seen in the building's high gables, round towers, steep conical roofs, and ornamental carvings. Also typical of this style was the use of smooth-faced gray Bedford stone (Indiana limestone) in its construction.

To create the asymmetrical, castle-like appearance the architects incorporated three large circular turrets, five chimneys and fourteen flues. Short columns with classical motifs and broad arches were also used to produce this form. All masonry work on the building was done by Bengt Aronson, a contractor from Minneapolis. The stone carvings and decorations were created by sculptor Herman Schlink. The mansion took several years to complete and the Turnblads moved in around 1908.

The Turnblad residence under construction, circa 1907.

Design Elements: Turnblad's Influence

At the turn of the century it was routine to have the architectural firm design the interiors as well as the exterior, of the home. However, in the case of Turnblad's mansion, he clearly made many of the building's design decisions himself. Turnblad's decorating ideas were drawn from a variety of sources, particularly architectural design books, catalogs, and from visits to manor homes on his many European trips. This is the reason for the diversified design elements of the mansion's interior. Many of the designs on the ceilings and walls can be traced directly to architectural sample books that belonged to Turnblad. One such book, *Ornamentets Bok,* was published in Stockholm, Sweden in 1900. It contains color plates of various ornamental motifs from around the world. The most obvious example can be seen in the carved griffins located at the base of the Grand Hall stairs. These griffins are nearly identical to a drawing of the same creature depicted in *Ornamentets Bok.*

Turnblad's personal and eclectic tastes can be found throughout the house. Motifs frequently found in the mansion were not merely superficial emblems common to the times but were symbols that held deeply rooted meaning for this Swedish immigrant. The griffin, mentioned above, is a legendary creature that is believed to have protected the gold of the Scythians in Greek mythology. It represents both lion and eagle and has been artistically depicted in varying combinations of these two real-life animals.

Around the mansion the griffin can be seen carved in stone on the exterior, carved in wood on the staircase, sculpted in plaster on the ceilings, molded in tile on the porcelain tile stoves and carved on much of the Turnblad furniture.

Carved griffin at the base of Grand Hall staircase. One of many griffins that appear throughout the Turnblad estate.

A griffin is shown in relief on a tile stove located in a second floor chamber.

The head and wings of a griffin are carved on the exterior of the building.

A wooden settee, made in 1895 for Swan Turnblad, shows his interest in the mythical griffin.

It is probable that either consciously or subconsciously the griffin symbolized the two countries that were so important to Turnblad; both his former homeland, Sweden, and his adopted land, America. The lion represents the Swedish symbol found on the Royal coat of arms, and the eagle embodies the American national emblem. These two symbols combined into one figure form the two halves that united Turnblad's life.

Woodwork

The interior of the mansion contains 33 rooms, and each is as ornamentally appointed as the exterior. Most notable is the extensive carving in the dining room, music room, and grand hall. Turnblad imported exotic wood species such as African and Honduran mahogany that grew in virgin forests, and were rarely seen in homes at this time. It was not until after 1915 that these woods began to appear in the more grand estates in the Midwest. Other more common wood types such as quarter-sawn white oak and American walnut are also found throughout the mansion. Oral history tells us that eighteen wood carvers from Aaron Carlson and Sons company were employed for two years to execute the elaborate work. Some of the carving was done at the shop and later installed in the mansion and some was carved on the premises.

Plasterwork

The interior plaster sculpture that adorns almost every room in the mansion was executed in 1905. It was common practise at the time to select patterns for the plasterwork from catalogs from which the architect would draw the chosen design to scale. Unpainted factory-made casts were commonly fitted together in sections. Turnblad selected many of the plaster designs from the Swedish architectural books that he owned. It is likely that he then had Herman Schlink (the stone carver

Detail of Rococo Revival plaster ceiling design in the Salon.

and plaster designer hired by Turnblad) draw the design to scale and to act as foreman for the plasterworkers.

To create the plaster ornamentation the "inverse" technique was used. This was done by first carving the molds for the designs from hardwood, usually boxwood, and they were then oiled to facilitate the removal of the plaster cast. After the first layer of plaster was poured, horsehair was laid in the plaster for strength. Then the last coats of plaster were poured to seal in the horsehair fibers. (Today hemp is used in place of horsehair.) The plaster molds were then situated on the ceiling by applying wet plaster to the area and positioning the cast forms in place. Among the ceiling motifs that are found in the mansion are griffins, angels, and intricate floral patterns. Many of the sculpted ceilings were then painted in a wide variety of colors.

Multi-colored sculpted ceilings were popular at the turn of the century and Turnblad's mansion boasted an impressive array of them. Not all the ceilings in the home were painted. Some of them were left uncolored as though they were never finished; this is especially true of rooms located on the second floor. It is reasonable to assume that Turnblad had intended to finish them because the ceilings are appointed with decorative plaster work, which at that time was usually painted. He would have polychromed the less important areas last.

In the 1930s many of the museum's colored ceilings were painted white. During this time the ornate original color scheme was out of fashion and it was popular to have white monochromatic ceilings. Since the 1970s, restoration work has been in progress to return the rooms, as closely as possible, to the original. This is a difficult task, because the historical records are sketchy. Consequently, it is necessary to determine the original colors and designs through historical photographs, early documents and many paint scrapings taken from the ceilings.

Porcelain Tile Stoves (Kakelugnar)

The eleven porcelain tile stoves comprise a prominent feature of the mansion's interior. These stoves, called *kakelugnar* (plural) in Swedish, are combinations of fireplaces and heating stoves. Swedish *kakelugnar* were unmatched anywhere for their beauty, high efficiency and graceful elegance. Seven of the *kakelugnar* in the house were made at the Uppsala-Ekeby Porcelain Factory in Uppsala, between 1897 and 1904. Two stoves were made at the Rörstrand Porcelain Company and there are two that are unidentified as to the source. The stoves were transported in sections and later assembled in the rooms of the Turnblad estate.

A delicate porcelain tile stove on the second floor.

Historically, the tile stove was first developed in Germany in the 15th century. Smoke from the fire travels up and down a series of vertical passages inside the stove. As gases move through the passages they heat up the masonry and warmth radiates into the room after the damper is closed. This heating source saved tremendously on the amount of fuel needed to warm a dwelling. A small fire built in an open grate in the base of the stove is sufficient to last the day.

In the 17th century Sweden began making tile stoves. Manufacture continued into the early 20th century at which time 43 different factories were still producing *kakelugnar* and employing about 1500 workers.[16] By about 1910 production slackened when modern furnaces made the stoves obsolete. Turnblad purchased his *kakelugnar* between 1904 and 1907, collecting his tile stoves in the period when their production in Sweden was beginning to wane.

Turnblad's collection of *kakelugnar* is unrivaled in the United States. They differ in color and style and each was chosen to coordinate with the colors and designs of a particular room. No two stoves are alike. Some have nickel firebox covers with ornate protruding handles; others have arched or squared decorated brass double doors. Turnblad limited his selection to Renaissance Revival and Rococo Revival designs, with classic motifs such as shells, fleur-de-lis, and floral patterns. Several of the stoves have large mirrors above the mantel ledges, a popular feature in the late 19th century.

The stoves were design elements and not intended to heat the building, because Turnblad had installed central heating with thermostats to control the temperature on each floor. At the turn of the century, central heating was not yet in common use and he was one of the first in the area to install it in his home, another example of his progressive ideas.

A whimsical porcelain tile stove with supporting figures and bas-relief panel.

One of many ornate thermostat covers found throughout the mansion.

Artisans/Craftsmen for the Turnblad Mansion

Ulrich Steiner, Master Woodcarver

Ulrich Steiner was born in Berne, Switzerland in 1879, and was one of a family of twelve children. Steiner's father was a woodcarver in Berne and it was here that his son, Ulrich, served a four-year apprenticeship. During his apprenticeship, two days a week were set aside for drawing and modeling and four days per week for carving. After completion of his training he worked an additional four years at various shops in Berne. In 1902, at age 23, Steiner emigrated to the United States. He first lived in La Crosse, Wisconsin, and, in 1905, settled in Minneapolis where he lived until his death in 1977. During the period that he worked on the Turnblad mansion he was employed by Aaron Carlson and Sons, a cabinet-making company in Minneapolis.[17]

Steiner was 26 when he first started working on the Turnblad mansion. He recalled that he was paid a higher wage than the other woodcarvers hired by Aaron Carlson. The other woodcarvers were paid 40 cents an hour for their work while he was paid five cents more per hour.[18] Examples of Steiner's work can be seen in the extensively carved dining room ceiling and walls, where it is believed that he also designed and carved most of the furniture, including the sideboard and a table that accommodates 24 people. He is best known for his fruit and flower motifs and these can be seen throughout the dining room in the form of the Della Robia wreaths. These wreaths encircle the chandelier above the carved dining table and the fireplace. He was also responsible for carving the intricate bas-relief within the wreath on the fireplace. This carving depicts a scene from a Swedish legend in which two trolls have spirited a maiden away from her earthly home to their enchanted world. The carving is called *Den bergtagen* or "the one spirited into the mountain." It has been adopted as the official seal of the American Swedish Institute.

In addition to carving the dining room, Ulrich Steiner carved the griffins located on the main staircase, as well as the fifty-two cherubs in the music room. Each cherub has different wings: some are adorned with insect wings, or angel wings, and others have butterfly, bird, or dragonfly wings. After the music room was completed, Steiner is reported to have stated that he never wanted to carve another cherub again.

Wood relief carving on Dining Room fireplace.

Detail of the Music Room fireplace with cherub carved from Honduran mahogany.

Albin Polasek, Wood Sculptor

The two-story African mahogany fireplace that decorates the Grand Hall was designed and carved by Albin Polasek (1879–1965). Polasek, born in Frenstat, Moravia, Czechoslovakia on February 14, 1879, came to the United States as a youth and worked as a woodcarver in La Crosse, Wisconsin. Here he met and first worked with Ulrich Steiner. In the summer of 1906, Polasek came to Minneapolis where he was hired to carve "a mahogany mantel with caryatids and other elaborate decorations. Here he was delighted to find Ulrich Steiner, the Swiss woodcarver from La Crosse, at work in the same factory."[19] (This refers to Aaron Carlson and Sons factory.)

An oral history from some of the original workmen stated that Polasek started and completed in one week's time the two large male figures that support the fireplace. It was once remembered that he was given the unlikely amount of $1,000 for each of the figures, which he called "Barbarians."[20] However, according to Ruth Sherwood in her biography of Polasek, he was offered three dollars a day for his work but instead asked to be paid by the foot because he could carve

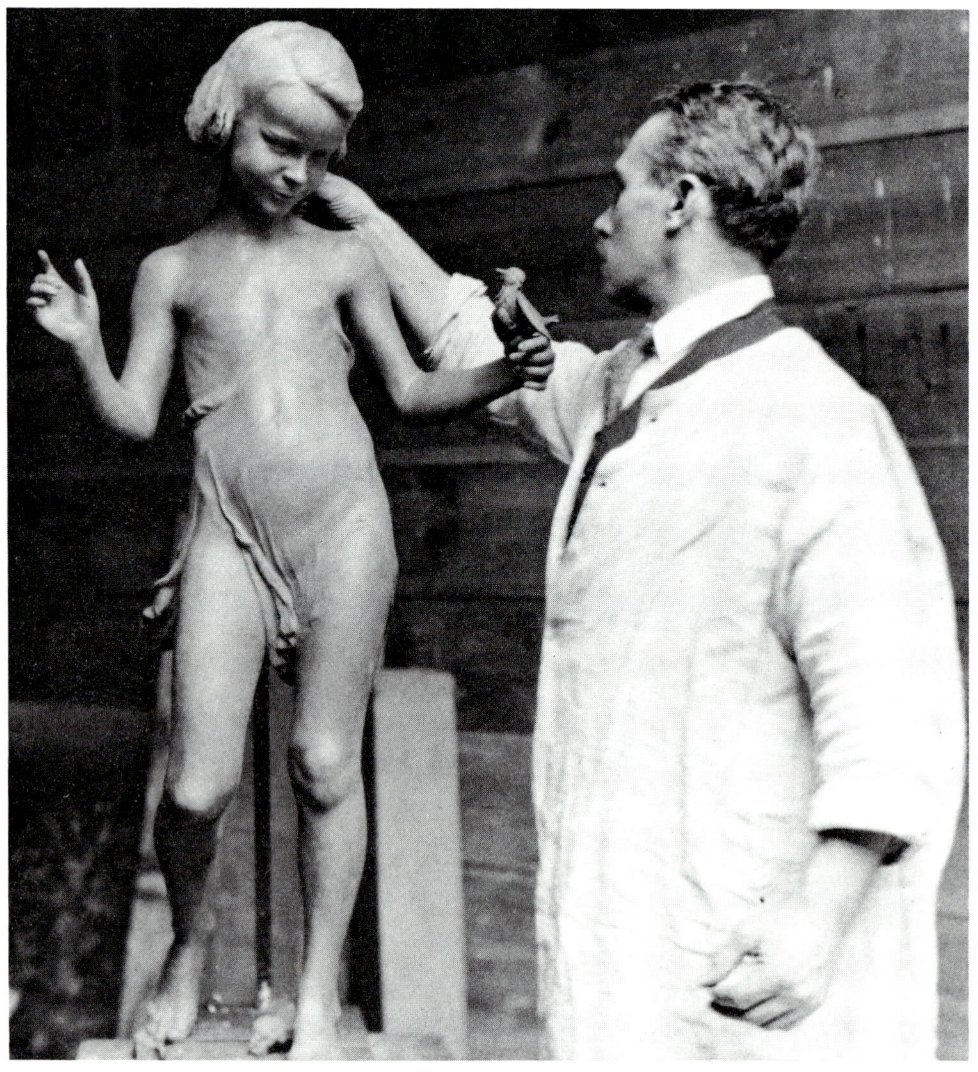

Albin Polasek, the wood sculptor who carved the Grand Hall fireplace. He is pictured here with one of his sculptures created when he was at the Art Institute of Chicago.

Detail of the herm figure that was called a "Barbarian" by its carver, Albin Polasek.

so quickly. (He was paid $7.50 per foot for statutes up to three feet; he was paid $10.00 per foot for statues over six feet.) The barbarian figures were made from slabs of African mahogany that had been glued together. The wood was hewn to acquire the general form and then finished with fine woodworking tools. It has been reported that after the figures were completed they were rubbed with a mixture of linseed oil and rotten stone, thus giving them the high polish that makes them distinct.[21]

After his work on the Turnblad mansion, Polasek studied at the Pennsylvania Academy of Fine Art and the American Academy in Rome. After numerous international awards for his sculpture, he became the director of sculpture training at the Art Institute of Chicago.

Herman Schlink, Stone Carver and Plaster Designer

Herman G. Schlink (1869–1950) was the architectural stone sculptor and plaster designer for the Turnblad mansion. During the construction of the building, Schlink created all the interior plaster decorations and the exterior stone carvings on the mansion and carriage house. Schlink was born in Winona, Minnesota in 1869 and came to Minneapolis as a youth. He studied at the Chicago Art Institute and then returned to Minneapolis. At age 36 he began work on the Turnblad mansion. After completing this job he continued to work in the city until his death on August 5, 1950.

Herman Schlink working on a plaster sculpture of a lion's head. It is possibly a prototype of the stone gargoyles around the exterior of the mansion.

During an interview in 1955, Mrs. Schlink, widow of Herman, said that her husband had been instructed by Swan J. Turnblad to carve the fourteen lions' heads on the building's exterior as grotesquely as possible. She also reported that when Schlink completed his work with the stone carving on the building and was packing up to leave, Swan Turnblad called him back to make a sculptured head of a horse for the carriage house. Because Mr. Schlink did not have a model he was reluctant to undertake the project. Turnblad insisted and Schlink extemporaneously created the well-shaped, spirited horse's head that still adorns the historic carriage house.[22]

Bengt Aronson, Stone Mason

The man who was hired to lay the limestone block for Turnblad's massive stone structure was Bengt Aronson (1845–1922). Aronson and his brother Louis were born in Sweden and emigrated to America in 1867 and 1870, respectively. They came to Minneapolis in 1872 and began a stone and brick business in 1884. They started as masons and later became contractors. Their buildings had the reputation of being the finest in the city, and it was reported in *The Minneapolis Morning Tribune* that the Aronsons did all the masonry work on the Minneapolis Court House, the first three floors of the Guaranty Loan Building in Minneapolis (no longer standing), and many other buildings in this area including the Glass Block, (known as the Donaldson Building), and Temple Court, demolished in 1953. Aronson also built Dania Hall, located on Cedar Avenue and 5th Street in Minneapolis. The brothers were considered "Minneapolis' biggest contractor" and they were awarded the contracts for most of the important local buildings.[23]

Sculpted limestone horse's head above the carriage house entrance.

III. The Museum: An Ethnic Mission

In 1929 Swan Johan Turnblad wrote in the ASI's Articles of Incorporation that his former estate would be used as a public institution for the sole purpose of education to advance instruction in and knowledge of Swedish arts, literature, and science. He held in high regard both his Swedish heritage and the land to which he had immigrated. Turnblad envisioned the institute as a melding of the two countries and he was quoted as saying, "It has been my lifelong ambition to foster and preserve Swedish culture in America."[24] These views were the basis for the museum's founding.

Through the years the ASI has evolved to include the preservation of Swedish-American history and culture, as well as the maintenance of ties to Sweden. Today the museum's mission is to collect artifacts that relate to the lifestyles of the Swedish-American in the Midwest, specifically during the most active period of Swedish immigration from 1845–1930. An important focus of the museum are Swedish customs and activities, both past and present, that are entrenched in the cultural heritage in the Midwest.

The purpose of the museum is fulfilled by collecting, preserving, and exhibiting Swedish and Swedish-American materials through interpretive exhibits, both permanent and temporary, educational programs, lectures, conferences, concerts and classes. These efforts all help to create an understanding of the establishment and contributions of immigrant Swedes in the Midwest.

One of the museum's primary ways of educating is through interpretative exhibits that are installed on three floors of the historic building. The separate floors define the three distinctive exhibition areas. On display on the first floor are recently restored turn-of-the-century period rooms, many of which are appointed with furniture and decor that reflect the rooms' individual design motifs. Since the Turnblads left very little furniture, most of what is now displayed has been acquired by the museum through the years. Included in the period rooms are a salon or drawing room that is an interpretation of a Rococo interior, a Moorish-inspired smoking room, an extensively carved dining room, a music room and a breakfast room that is a recreation of an 18th century Swedish manor house room.

The museum's second floor also contains period rooms, including a library and a den. The rooms that served as former bedchambers are now used as gallery spaces for temporary exhibits. Typical exhibits consist of contemporary Swedish and Swedish-American art, immigration history exhibits, and special displays from the museum's permanent collection.

The third floor of the historic building features the powerful story of Swedish immigration and settlement in Minnesota. It is a story told through the physical belongings that accompanied the immigrants when they came to America and objects that they created to help them adapt to their new environment. Artifacts on exhibit include *Amerika* trunks, eating and cooking utensils, clothing, textiles, weaving implements, tools and equipment, family memorabilia, including Swedish bibles, family photographs and diaries.

The ASI is a living history museum. It is a place where guides dressed in Swedish folk costumes conduct tours, and demonstrations of Swedish traditions such as folk dancing, handcrafts, and food customs are regularly scheduled. At certain times during the year the museum hosts story tellers who convey Swedish customs through legends and myths, as well as having animated performers who dramatize the lives of Swedish and Swedish-American historical figures. These are some of the methods used by the museum to create an understanding of the Swedish-Americans' ethnic past, and a sense of living history.

The Grand Hall features a richly-carved two-story mahogany fireplace. Porcelain urns with an elephant motif were purchased by Swan Turnblad from Rörstrand Porcelain Company in Sweden. Paintings from the museum's collection are displayed on the walls.

IV. The Historic Mansion: Room by Room

Grand Hall staircase.

The Grand Hall

The Grand Hall is paneled and embellished in fine-grained, African mahogany. A two-story fireplace carved in this same exotic wood is the room's central focus. It was designed and carved by the internationally accredited sculptor, Albin Polasek. Supporting the fireplace mantel are two herm figures, draped in animal hides, that are referred to as "Barbarians" by their carver. In the center are two female figures leaning on a clock between them. The sculptures represent the passing of time. The figure on the left portrays night with her eyes closed and a symbol of a moon in her hand. The one on the right signifies day with her eyes open and butterflies alighting on her hair. Resting on the top of the fireplace is the bust of a male figure believed to be a Viking. The stone that surrounds the face of the fireplace opening is white onyx.

Also located in the Grand Hall are two griffins that rest at the base of the ornate staircase. The griffin is a mythological figure that is composed of both eagle and lion. It is evident that Turnblad selected this figure from an architectural design book and had woodcarver Ulrich Steiner (1879–1977) carve it in African mahogany. The griffins' outstretched paws may represent a welcoming gesture to guests.

Artwork by Swedish and Swedish-American artists is displayed on the walls in the Grand Hall. A portrait of the ASI founder, painted by Christian von Schneidau, is located in this area.

The porcelain urns that flank the fireplace were manufactured at Rörstrand Porcelain Company in Sweden. They were purchased by Turnblad in the early 20th century.

The Salon

A room commonly found in mansions built at the turn of the century was the salon. In the Turnblad home it is a rectangular room with a light-colored interior that is an interpretation of Rococo style, an 18th century artistic form characterized by fancifully curved shapes and ornamental shellwork. It was restored to its original appearance in 1975 by Gertrude Gump, a specialist in interior restoration. The wool carpets were designed specifically for the room.

The salon is used to display temporary exhibits from the ASI's decorative arts collection.

The Salon is a light-colored room decorated in Rococo Revival style. Wool carpets were woven to fit the shape of this rectangular room.

Historic photograph of Den with original wall and ceiling fixtures. The ASI Museum Gift Shop is presently located in this room.

The Den

Another room common to the time period of the mansion is the den. This room was executed in Moorish or Arabic-style decor. These influences are exemplified in the ogival or onion-shaped domes carved in the doors, and the geometric and plant patterns on the ceiling and walls. The Arabic script that was carved into the original wooden pillars and the wooden freize carvings, seen in the historic photograph of the room, were removed in the 1940s. It is possible that the freize was cut out of wood and fastened to existing wooden pegs that were embedded in the walls. Other elements that are repeated throughout the room are the gilded raised bands and borders of the ceiling.

The decorative motifs on the ceiling and walls can be traced to an architectural sample book that belonged to Swan Turnblad, called *Ornamentets Bok*. It is evident that Turnblad selected the ornamental motifs from this book because elements from the Moorish section are identical to patterns used in the den.

Of the many features of the den, the most salient is the porcelain tile stove. The colors and design of the stove are compatible with the features of the room. It was once thought that Lillian Turnblad had designed the *kakelugn;* however, research indicates that it was designed by E. H. Tryggelin and manufactured at Rörstrand Porcelain Company in Stockholm, Sweden in 1895.[25] The stove pattern appears in a Rörstrand catalog dating from this time and it is likely that Lillian selected the motif from this catalog.

To maintain historical accuracy the den was restored to its original colors in the summer of 1986 when the initial paint colors were uncovered from the room's walls and ceiling by Marvin A. Anderson and Curt Pederson, specialists in historic restoration. Today a Moorish-inspired stenciled wall design appears in place of the original wall pillars and fixtures that had been removed in the 1940s. Also removed from the room at this same time was an ornate Moorish design chandelier, which was given to the Shrine Temple by Lillian Turnblad. The ASI Museum Gift Shop is currently located in this room.

The Dining Room

The most elaborately carved room in the historic house is the dining room. Carvings of flowers, fruit and wreaths appear extensively in the oak and bleached Honduran mahogany. Ulrich Steiner designed and carved the furniture and the panels on the walls and ceiling.

The table is believed to have been carved in place and, when extended, it corresponds to the shape of the room. It is square on one end and semi-circular on the other.

A unique feature in the dining room is the built-in carved sideboard. Special features of it are the concave and convex glass doors. The drawers are wedge-shaped with rounded corners which afforded the maximum use of space. Inside the sideboard the Turnblad china is displayed. The formal "Empire" pattern was made by Rörstrand Porcelain Company in Stockholm, Sweden. It was one of the most exquisite and expensive services made at that time. On the back of each piece, inscribed in gold, appears the name "Swan J. Turnblad" and "2600 Park Avenue."

The large fireplace is positioned between two hand-carved benches. Two carved female figures (called caryatids) support the mantelpiece. Marble used on the face of the fireplace is from Kolmården, Sweden.

The intricately patterned wool rugs were made to complement the complex design of the room's wood carvings.

View of the Dining Room with its heavily paneled walls and ceiling. Coordinating furniture in the room was carved in place.

Ceiling detail showing an example of a Della Robia wreath, in the Dining Room.

The built-in sideboard of oak and mahogany features convex and concave glass panels.

The Turnblad's personal china was made by the Rőr-strand Company, Sweden. The "Empire" pattern was produced from 1902 until 1908 and was their most luxurious service at the time.

Relief carving of Den Bergtagen, *a Swedish legend.*

View of the Dining Room fireplace with built-in side benches.

The Breakfast Room

Stylistically, this room is a dramatic departure from the other rooms in the mansion. The walls and ceiling of the breakfast room were restored, by Gertrude Gump, to their original colors, but the furnishings were chosen to replicate a room from a Swedish manor house in the 18th century. The furniture from the room is known as "Gustavian" style and was acquired from Sweden specifically for the room. (Gustavian refers to a design that dates 1770–1810 and was named after Swedish King Gustav III. It was a Swedish modification of the French Louis XVI style.)

The *kakelugn* in this room is a Rococo Revival style that was produced at the Rörstrand Porcelain Company in Stockholm, Sweden. It is said to have won first prize at the Paris Exposition of 1900.

The painting displayed in this room, a portrait of a woman, has been suggested by scholars to have allegorical references to the Mary Magdalene. It was created by the first nationally-acclaimed Swedish-American painter, Gustaf (Gustavus) Hesselius (1682–1755). After receiving an education in art in Stockholm, Sweden, he left in 1711 and travelled to London, seeking a passport to go to America. In 1712, after being recommended for a passport by Governor William Penn, Hesselius reached his destination of Fort Christina in Delaware. He painted religious scenes and portraits and is well known for his depictions of famous figures in the 1700s, including the Lenape Indian chiefs Lapowinsa and Tishcohan, and Governor Patrick Gordon.

The Breakfast Room is decorated as a room from an 18th century Swedish manor house.

The Music Room

The function for which this room was designed is unmistakable in its theme. Here Ulrich Steiner carved lyres to adorn the squared, heavy pillars. Delicately colored musical instruments appear in relief in the plastered ceiling of the alcove. The acoustical qualities of the room have been acknowledged by area musicians, as it has historically accommodated numerous recitals and musical programs.

The woodwork in the music room includes large pillars that support carved friezes, where a variety of cherubs appear each with a different type of wing. Carved garlands connect the cherubs around the room. Woodwork in the room was made by Ulrich Steiner, from Honduran mahogany, a variety not typically used during the early 20th century.

The ceiling and walls in this room were polychromed by Marvin A. Anderson between 1980–1981. Originally they had been painted a solid color.

The original historic carpet seen here was ordered by Turnblad in the early 1900s. Oral history states that the rugs were made of Swedish wool but woven on looms in Austria, because Swedish looms were too small to create such large rugs. (The rugs for the entire house reportedly cost $51,000 dollars.)[26]

The paintings in this room include portraits of Swedish kings. One famous work is an 18th century portrait of Swedish King Gustav III (1746–1792) that was created by Per Krafft the Elder (1724–1793).

Music Room with carved mahogany freize and ornate fireplace.

The Visby Window

Located above the Grand Hall stairs is the prominent stained glass window commonly called the "Visby Window." The scene on the window is a copy of a painting, titled, "Valdemar Atterdag Levying Contributions on Visby," by Swedish artist Carl Gustaf Hellquist (1851–1890), owned by the National Museum in Stockholm, Sweden. It depicts an episode from history in which the Danish king Valdemar Atterdag is sacking the city of Visby, on the island of Gotland, Sweden in 1361, a Hanseatic town in the Baltic. In the narrative scene the citizens of Visby are shown reluctantly bringing their treasures and placing them in large casks located in the town's square. In return for the riches the Danish king (seated on the dias) has promised to spare the citizens and their town.

The window was created by the Neumann and Vogel Glass Company of Stockholm in 1908. It is made from hand-blown glass that has been painted or stained with an oil-based fused-on enamel. Individual pieces of stained glass were cut out and fitted together, much like an enormous jig-saw puzzle. Lead caming holds the multitude of cut glass pieces in place to form the overall scene. The remarkable transparency and clarity of color is a distinctive feature of the window.

Solarium

An unusual architectural feature of the mansion is the copper-roofed solarium, which is situated directly above the porte cochere. This room is surrounded by windows and has a built-in bench that wraps around its interior. In the 18th and early 19th centuries solariums were used for displaying plants and as a sitting room in winter.

The Visby Window is a stained glass window that depicts a scene from a famous painting by Swedish artist Carl Gustaf Hellquist, called "Valdemar Atterdag Levying Contributions on Visby."

Second Floor

The Library

The bookcase-lined library is paneled in bleached American walnut, a commonly used wood native to the Midwest. The bookcases contain books from Swan Turnblad's personal collection, the J. B. Gans library, as well as other book collections given to the ASI.

A special feature in the room is the dark-hued tile stove. Research indicates that stoves of this style were manufactured at three factories in Sweden: *Sandbäcks Kakelugnsfabrik* in Kalmar circa 1889, *Karlskrona Kakelugnfabrik,* circa 1900, and *Uppsala-Ekeby Kakelugnsfabrik* in Uppsala, circa 1900. The Turnblad stove could have come from any of the three factories; however, it is probable that it came from Uppsala-Ekeby, where most of the other tile stoves in the mansion were purchased.

Library with built-in bookcases and tile stove. (The table was given by Swan Johan Turnblad.)

The relief panel on the tile stove depicts a scene from the life of Emperor Charles V, King of Spain and the Netherlands. In the scene, which takes place in Augsburg circa 1520, Charles V is visiting Jakob Fugger, one of Europe's wealthiest merchants, who had loaned the Emperor a great deal of money. Fugger had accumulated a large number of signed notes from the king, and to display his great wealth he destroyed them by throwing them into the fire built with cinnamon bark, an exotic and expensive spice at the time.[27]

It is believed that the multi-colored plaster ceiling in the library still bears its original paint. Currently the shades are muted because of fading due to excessive cleaning, age and exposure to sunlight through the years.

Portraits of Christina, Swan and Lillian Turnblad adorn the north wall of the library. They were painted by Sister Marie Teresa in the late 1930s. She was the head of the art department at the College of St. Catherine in St. Paul and later took up residence at The Academy of the Holy Angels in Minneapolis. It was while Sister Teresa was here that she painted the family portraits. (Lillian Turnblad was a resident of the Academy from 1934 until her death in 1943.) The portraits of Christina and Swan were painted post mortem.

Detail of bas-relief panel on the Library's tile stove.

Historic photograph of Library, circa 1930s.

 Historic photograph of the Sitting Room, circa 1930s.

Den/Reading Room
(First Chamber)

Bookcases installed in this room were originally from Turnblad's Posten Building. The black leather chair once belonged to Swan Turnblad. The tile stove was manufactured in Uppsala, at the *Uppsala-Ekeby Kakelugnsfabrik*. The ceiling in this room was painted in the same colors as those in the library; presumably they were painted at the same time.

Second Chamber/Glass Room

This room is one of the five rooms identified as "chambers" on the original blueprint. The *kakelugn* in this room was made in Uppsala, and is a Rococo Revival design.

The ceiling and walls were painted by Marvin A. Anderson and Curt Pederson in the early 1980s, the colors having been taken from those appearing on the porcelain stove. Today this room is used as an exhibit area for the museum's extensive collection of historic and contemporary Swedish glass.

Third Chamber

The third chamber functions more as a passageway than as a chamber, although at one time it may have been used as a dressing room. A closet and a bathroom are situated behind the mirrored mahogany doors in this area. The position of the bathroom would have been appropriate because it linked two of the largest bedchambers on the second floor. A delicate shell design is found on the tile stove in this area. Currently, it serves as a gallery for temporary exhibitions.

Fourth Chamber/Sitting Room

This room was also designated as a "chamber" on the original blueprints and probably served as both a sitting room and bed chamber. It is unknown how the Turnblads furnished it because there are no existing photographs that show it fully appointed. It is quite possible that the room served as a private bedroom for Mr. and Mrs. Turnblad.

One of six kakelugnar *found on the second floor of the museum.*

The chamber/sitting room is an example of Art Nouveau decorative style, typical of the late 19th century. This popular design can be seen in the historic carpet with its bold, sinuous lines that takes a departure from the more traditional design motifs found in the mansion's other carpets. The blue hues are repeated in this room's *kakelugn,* produced at the Uppsala-Ekeby porcelain factory.

Since no restoration work has yet been done in this chamber it is unknown if the ceiling was originally polychromed like many of the others in the building.

Today this room serves as a gallery for temporary exhibits both from the ASI museum collection and other sources.

Fifth Chamber/Lillian Turnblad Room

Adjacent to the large chamber is a small room with delicate plasterwork, believed to have been the former bedchamber of the daughter, Lillian Turnblad. During the restoration in 1988, executed by Marvin A. Anderson and Curt Pederson, it was discovered that the ceiling had never been painted in the traditional polychromed style. At the turn of the century an ornamental plaster ceiling would probably not have remained unpainted. Thus, it is reasonable to assume that this chamber was never finished and only the primer coat of paint was applied.

As part of the restoration project, the ceiling has been painted to reflect the common early 20th century decorative style. Colors for the ceiling were taken from those found in the room's tile stove, composed of subdued shades of pink, green and yellow that highlight the elegant Rococo Revival design.

Originally, a bathroom was located behind the mahogany door inside the room. Large portieres hung in front of the entrance into the large chamber/sitting room. Today this room functions as an exhibition area.

The Värmland Room

Third Floor

Ballroom

The Turnblad family rarely entertained guests in their home, despite the opulent facilities built for such activities. In fact, there was only one documented function held at the Turnblad home. The event took place in 1921 and was a celebration of the Aero Club. (This club was founded in 1917, to recruit pilots for World War I.) Several hundred people were invited and as reported in the *Minneapolis Morning Tribune,* it was the "first time the estate had been thrown open to any residents of Minneapolis."[28]

Today the ballroom is used occasionally for plays that are performed on the proscenium-style stage; however, the primary purpose of the room is to display interpretive exhibitions about Swedish immigration and life in Swedish-America.

The lives of Swedish settlers and early immigrants are shown through the exhibits displayed in the ballroom and lounge areas. Practical everyday objects that were needed both on the journey to America and in settling rural communities can be seen here. *Amerika* trunks, food chests, bibles, tools, household articles and family heirlooms are some of the historic objects that help to interpret the immigrant experience and heighten awareness of this on-going process.

The Ballroom with a proscenium-style stage.

Studio/The Värmland Room

Oral history reveals that this room was originally used as an artist's studio for Lillian Turnblad. When she painted, she favored the natural light provided by the room's skylights and many windows. Now the room houses the "Värmland Gift"; a collection of objects from all the parishes in Värmland, Sweden. The gift was made in 1952 and contains more than one hundred and fifty articles that best represented each of the communities in this province. In the 19th century many immigrants from Värmland settled in Minnesota and this gift symbolizes the continuing connection between Värmland and Minnesota.

Turnblad had originally planned this Studio for his daughter to pursue her artistic interests. The room now houses the Värmland Collection.

The Weaving Room

A significant segment of the museum's collection consists of handwoven textiles and weaving implements that date from the mid to late 19th century. In the 19th century, before a family left Sweden to make the trip to America, many handwoven clothes and textiles were produced specifically for this journey. These historic textiles make up the core of the museum's nationally-known textile collection. Many of these historic objects are displayed in the weaving room. To continue this age-old handcraft tradition, Swedish weaving classes and demonstrations are offered at the ASI Museum.

A spinning wheel from the museum's collection.

Auditorium

As a museum and cultural center, the American Swedish Institute hosts many ethnic events. To accommodate these activities, a large auditorium was built in 1983. It is here that many Swedish and Swedish-American traditions are celebrated and customs observed. A painted mural on the walls of the auditorium tells the story of emigration by Swedes to America and their settlement in Minnesota. The pictorial story also highlights Swedish traditions that have been preserved in America.

The mural was painted by Swedish artist Bengt Engman (1925–1987), a fourth generation "Dala" folk painter who specialized in the traditional artistic style called *Dalmålning*. The name *Dalmålning* is derived from the Swedish province of Dalarna where this type of painting was commonly found.

In the 19th century, Swedish itinerant folk painters would decorate walls and ceilings of peasants' homes with this charming artistic style. Often themes for the scenes were biblical verses. Narratives that told of family or community events, or histories and stories, were also used. The narrative or story form is the basis of the folk painting in the auditorium.

Detail of a Bengt Engman (1925–1987) mural.

Closed Areas

Commonly asked questions by museum visitors are: "Where is the kitchen?," "Where did the Turnblad's servants live?," "Are any of the former bathrooms on display?," "Why are these rooms unavailable to the public?"

Some areas in the historic house are not accessible to the public because they are needed to store the museum's collection, and to accommodate office space. However, in response to the frequently asked questions, a brief description of the inaccessible rooms, their original function and decor, and their current use is included here.

Kitchen/Butler's Pantry/ Servant's Sitting Room

The former kitchen, now used as a storage area, is a spacious room located on the first floor. None of the original fixtures remain in the room, with the exception of a built-in closet designed to house the "refrigerator" (as designated on the original blueprint from 1904). At the rear of the kitchen there is a back door entrance, originally serving as access for deliveries and servants' entrance. The walls are dressed in white variegated marble and the floor is tiled in a mosaic pattern.

Situated between the kitchen and breakfast room is a butler's pantry, fitted with built-in cupboards from floor to ceiling.

Adjoining the kitchen is a hallway identified on the blueprints as "Servants' Hall." A back staircase is found in the hall and leads both to the lower level and the upper floors. A room designated as the "Servants' Sitting Room," connects to the hall.

Seamstress' Quarters/Sewing Room

The "sewing room" or seamstress' quarters located on the second floor reflects a custom from an earlier era. This series of rooms was designed as both living and working quarters for a seamstress who would have stayed with the family while making their seasonal clothing.

Positioned in the front of this suite of connecting rooms is the sewing area that has a massive built-in mirror covering the wall. An anteroom with a marble sink connects the sewing room to the back bedchamber. A door in this back area leads to the servants' staircase and a closet. All ceilings in the room designated as the seamstress' quarters were delicately moulded in plaster. They were polychromed in the 1970s by Gertrude Gump.

It is unknown if the Turnblad family ever hired a seamstress to live at the mansion to custom-make their clothing. However, there is evidence to suggest that they purchased goods at a local retail store. In an oral history provided by Samuel Hokanson, who was employed by Turnblad in 1928, he states that he drove Christina and Lillian Turnblad to St. Paul where they shopped at Schuneman and Evans Inc. Today this suite serves as an office for the curatorial staff.

Bathrooms

Only one of seven original bathrooms is open for museum visitors to view. No bathrooms are located on the mansion's first floor. They are found only on the second and third levels of the Turnblad home. One bathroom that was situated on the lower level no longer exists. Three bathrooms are located on the second floor and each one adjoins a different bedchamber. These vary in size and decor. On the landing between the second and third floors there is a small half bathroom that is open to the public. It has functioning porcelain fixtures.

At the back of the house, on the third floor, a servants' bathroom is positioned between the three servants' rooms. Walls and floor in this room are lined with ceramic tile. All of the former servants' quarters, including the bathroom, have been reconditioned to house the museum's large artifact collection.

The largest of the bathrooms in the mansion is located on the third floor. It still contains the original porcelain, footed bathtub positioned directly beneath a large skylight. Ceramic tile lines the walls and floor of this room. It currently functions as a storage area for the museum's collection.

The Lower Level

Although there is public access to the mansion's lower level, its present appearance is drastically different from what it was originally. Except for two porcelain tile stoves and a small amount of oak paneling, very little remains of the earlier ornamentation.

Through the years the area has been changed to accommodate the service needs of the ASI. For practical reasons, the smaller rooms were enlarged to create the auditorium and lounge areas, and a large kitchen facility was installed. Later a coffee shop (*Kaffe Stuga*) was added, and most recently, a book store (*Bokhandel*) was established.

Originally, the lower level was divided into a "Billiard" room, "Smoking" room, "Vegetable" storage, "Laundry" area, and an oak paneled "Gymnasium." Also listed on the blueprint was a "Bathroom" and adjacent to it a "Wine Cellar."

Historic photograph of the former "Smoking Room" located on the lower level.

Historic photograph of the former assembly room located in the mansion's lower level.

V. The Museum's Growing Collection: Pieces of History

The ASI's primary function as a ethnic museum is to collect objects that explain the Swedish presence in the Midwest during the Swedish immigration period. It is the largest museum in America dedicated to carrying out this goal, and its collection of Swedish-American material culture represents a unique national treasure.

Artifacts, fine art, and archival materials have been acquired for the ASI museum collection since its inception in 1929. This includes the substantial core collection donated by the museum's founder, Swan Johan Turnblad. In recent years the museum has expanded its extensive collection by actively acquiring objects related to Swedish-Americana.

The composition of the museum's collection is broad and diversified. The primary focus is on the material culture of the Swedish-Americans and objects that reflect the immigrants' experiences. Included are necessities brought with the Swedish immigrants to the new world, usually utilitarian objects, as well as articles made by and for Swedish-American consumers. These reflect a perpetuation of interest in the Swedish heritage that persisted in the adopted land.

Another component of the ASI museum collection includes items relating to the Swan J. Turnblad family and objects that are stylistically compatible with the period rooms of the historic Turnblad mansion.

Articles, both historic and contemporary, that represent Swedish customs and reflect these transplanted traditions in this country are also a part of the ASI's holdings. These objects, such as provincial folk costumes, "Dala" paintings, and Swedish handcrafts, symbolize the important continuity of the re-lationship between Sweden and America, and exemplify the cultural ties that have been inherited.

Paintings, woodcarvings, Swedish art glass, porcelain and decorative textiles are just a few of the objects that make up the museum's holdings. Selections from this group adorn the walls of the historic mansion and decorate the numerous period rooms. The works of both Swedish and Swedish-American artists and artisans are represented.

The potpourri urn was used to hold a mixture of flower petals and spices that served to freshen a room. It was made in 1901 by the Rörstrand Porcelain Company of Sweden.

Finally, the ASI archives and library, which is located in the former carriage house, represents a large and important element of the Institute's holdings. The collection contains both published and unpublished materials relating to the immigrant heritage, as well as the records of the Turnblad family, Turnblad's newspaper, *Svenska Amerikanska Posten,* and records of the ASI. These holdings include books, documents, manuscripts, letters, photographs, and microfilms. The wealth of materials found in the archives and library has made the ASI a primary place to research individual family history and conduct studies on Swedish immigration and its impact in the Upper Midwest.

Each year the ASI has received numerous gifts of ethnic material culture. Through the years several major contributions involving hundreds of rare, historically significant objects have been made. The first of these a gift from the famous Swedish-American artist Gustaf Tenggren, in 1949. He was most noted for his animation work at the Disney Studios, including "Snow White and the Seven Dwarfs" and "Pinocchio." This large and important gift of 18th and 19th century Swedish material culture and decorative arts reflects the lives of Swedish peasants in the province of Dalarna just before the first waves of mass migration to America. The significance of these objects is in their ability to help us understand the culture that was, in part, transplanted to Minnesota. Many of the Dala folk traditions represented by the collection still persist today.

Materials from the ASI Archives and Library.

Another significant contribution made to the museum is the Värmland gift, received in 1952. It represents both historical and modern material culture of the Swedish province of Värmland. The collection is of particular significance to the many Minnesotans whose ancestors came from this province.

In 1976 the Hilma Berglund collection was given to the ASI Museum. Hilma Berglund was a prominent Swedish-American who served as a University of Minnesota professor and helped to found the Minnesota Weavers Guild. Included in the Berglund collection are weaving implements, textiles, artwork, personal journals, and several examples of the "Minnesota Loom." This unique loom was designed by the Berglund family and fabricated at the lumber company owned by the Berglund family. These artifacts reflect the influences of Swedish-Americans on the state's ethnic culture.

The most recent gift of prominence is that of the Harvard University Art Museums donation. This collection of early 19th century Swedish decorative arts and furniture was donated in 1987. It had been part of the Busch-Reisinger (under the auspices of the larger Harvard University Art Museums) museum's holdings since the 1950s. It is exhibited on the museum's third floor.

The museum is dependent on these important donations and acquisitions to fulfill its purpose. The collection provides the museum with the physical objects that help to interpret the Swedish immigrant past. They are collected for exhibition purposes, for the preservation of past ethnic folkways and traditions, and to serve as a research collection for scholars and the general public.

An immigrant trunk packed with personal belongings, ready for the transatlantic crossing to the New World. All artifacts are from the museum's collection.

Trunks

*The handmade, wooden immigrant trunk (*kista*) is a common artifact found in the ASI's collection. Trunks are a symbol of the physical and spiritual separation made by the Swedish immigrants when they left their homeland. Before they were used for containers that carried the immigrants' belongings on the transatlantic voyage to the New World, trunks were used as chests to store linens, textiles, and clothing. In Sweden during the 19th century, chests-of-drawers began replacing the trunk as the primary furniture for storage, although trunks were still widely used in Swedish homes even into the early 20th century.*

In making the journey to America, a typical trunk would have been packed with clothing, linens, bed coverlets, homespun fabric, a copper coffee pot, wooden household articles, forged tools, weaving implements, a rifle (if one was owned), Swedish Bible, family heirlooms, and a portrait of the family's ancestors.

Trunks often were decorated with folk paintings or embellished with wrought iron fittings. Many were identified on the front with the immigrant's destination. Trunks varied in size and shape, depending on the decision of the individual maker; some had domed lids and others were flat.

The wooden trunks were used by immigrants in the earlier waves of immigration from Sweden. These were replaced later by the factory-made steamer trunks that were more common in the late 1800s and early 1900s.

Wooden utensils

Wood was a material that was found in abundance in heavily-forested Sweden. It provided the common folk with a substance for creating objects of utility, objects that enabled them to adapt to their natural environment. Use of wood in making utilitarian articles reaches back thousands of years in Scandinavian history. Through generations the essence of wood's natural pliability has been discerned and understood. With little effort wood has been manipulated into useful forms and it lends itself to being carved, steamed and bent, grooved, hollowed-out, and shaved into the desired shape.

Wood was so plentiful that it became a source for the Swedish artisan who could not afford to use expensive materials in creating objects of beauty for the home. In the hands of the woodcarver, designs, both sophisticated and crude, have been created. Both the woodcarvers' techniques and the wooden objects themselves have been passed down through generations. When the Swedish immigrants came to the Midwest, they brought with them both skills in woodcarving and many of the wooden objects that had earlier been in their families and were important parts of their home environment. Many of these wooden objects are found in the ASI's collection.

Värmland crown

The use of the bridal crown is a distinctively Scandinavian custom, and one that is still practiced in Swedish and Swedish-American weddings. The Scandinavian ritual of using a crown in the wedding ceremony may have been derived from the practice of adorning the statue of the Madonna with a crown in churches during the Catholic period.[29] *The Värmland crown is a reproduction of the one found in the Cathedral of Karlstad. The crown is part of the Värmland gift.*

Copper utensils

The copper industry in Sweden has been important to the Swedish economy since ancient times. Articles made of copper have been fairly common since this early period. They were often packed in immigrant trunks that were brought to America. Usually the copper utensils included coffee pots, kettles, pans, molds, large tubs, flasks and a variety of containers. Because of the material's durability and its importance in cooking, many of these objects have survived and are well represented in the museum's collection.

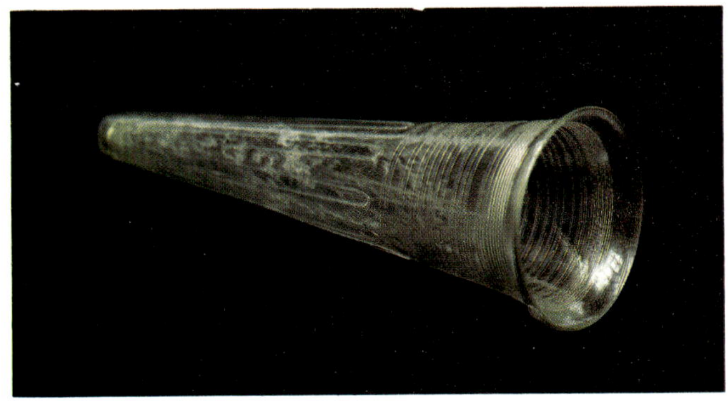

Ancient glass beaker

Authenticated and dated as late 5th or early 6th century A.D., *this flawless glass beaker is a rare artifact. It is the oldest and most rare object in the museum's collection. The beaker has been identified as a "Kempston" type vessel used as a glass for drinking.*[30] *Its conical shape and baseless feature illustrates a custom from an eariler era when drinking habits were quite different from what they are today.*[31] *Vessels of this type were found in the Rhineland, Northern France, Belgium, and England.*

Pewter

Pewter, a soft, malleable material composed largely of tin, was often used to create fine serving pieces such as these pitchers from the museum's collection. Objects of this quality were not often found among the Swedish immigrants' artifacts, but were collected by wealthy Swedish-Americans such as Swan J. Turnblad.

Bronze sculpture

This bronze sculpture was created by the internationally acclaimed Swedish artist Carl Milles (1875–1955). Milles is well known for his sculpture of the Mexican onyx Indian, called "Indian God of Peace," whose towering presence is found at the City Hall in St. Paul, Minnesota.

Bronze sculpture of girl

Paul Granlund (1925–) is an American sculptor who is best known for his figurative sculptures such as the depicted work "Balanced Figure," which is a part of the ASI's permanent collection of fine art.

Tools

During the first waves of migration from Sweden, tools often were brought by immigrants to this country. Later, letters that were sent back to Sweden from those who already had settled in this country advised those preparing to emigrate not to bring Swedish-made tools because better implements were available in the New World. The ASI's collection of tools is large and varied and includes such objects as carpentry tools, coopering tools, axes, shovels, and farming implements.

Oil painting

The museum has sought to collect art by important Swedish and Swedish-American artists and to chronicle their work and lives. This is an untitled landscape by Swedish-American artist Birger Sandzén (1871–1954).

Painted door

Pictured is a painted wooden door with portrait of Swedish Queen Christina, which dates to the 19th century. It is from the Gustaf Tenggren collection.

Woodcarvings

This woodcarving by the famous Swedish woodcarver Axel Petersson, also known as Döderhultarn (1868–1925), depicts a Swedish couple having their crying baby baptized by a minister.

Textile

The ASI's large textile collection is recognized nationally as being one of the largest assemblages of historic Swedish weaving. The collection consists of textiles that were brought to this country with the immigrants, as well as items woven here by Swedish-Americans. These textiles are important because they demonstrate the weave types, motifs, materials, and natural and commercially-made dyes that were used during the Swedish immigration period. Data such as this enables museum researchers to analyze how, and to what extent, these Swedish traditions were continued in this country, and how these techniques influenced weaving in the Midwest.

Ceramic pitcher

This ceramic pitcher was a gift in 1907 to Swan J. Turnblad from his wife, Christina and daughter, Lillian. It was made at the Rorstrand Porcelain Company in Sweden and depicts a Viking motif.

Silver ink well

Pictured is a Swedish silver ink well, circa 1860's, that once belonged to Carl Herman von Stockenström who worked as an Editor from 1896–1903 at the Svenska Amerikanska Posten newspaper. This object typifies the component of Turnblad memorabilia in the ASI's collection.

Dala painting

This Dalmålning *or folk painting from the province of Dalarna depicts a religious theme. Hjelt Per Persson (1821–1886) portrays a scene of the Nativity with Mary, Joseph and Jesus in the stable and the three wise men on the right. Note the figure above and left of the wise men which represents the angel that announced to the shepherds that a savior had been born. This style was common in the 19th century and was often found in the homes of peasants.*

Contemporary glass
Shown here are a glass vase and large plate by the Orrefors Glass Company, Småland, Sweden, from the large collection of Swedish contemporary glass in the museum's holdings.

VI. Cultural Center:
A Living Legacy

In addition to being an ethnic museum and historic mansion the Institute functions as a cultural center. It serves as a hub for regional activities that relate to Swedish history and Swedish-American cultural traditions. As part of the ASI's activities lectures, dramatic productions, dance recitals, films and musical programs are offered weekly.

To perpetuate the Swedish ethnic heritage the ASI offers classes in Swedish language, including the sponsorship of children's attendance at Sjölunden language camp. Classes in Swedish folk traditions such as folk dancing, "Dala" painting, weaving and other Swedish handcrafts are taught at the Institute.

In addition to offering classes, the ASI cultural groups help to perpetuate the Swedish heritage. The Swedish fiddling group (*Spelmanslag*) and large Male Chorus keep Swedish songs and music traditions alive. A folk dancing group for adults and Junior Folk Dancers for the young, are also important parts of the cultural center's activities.

Members of Spelmanslag, *a folk fiddling group, play Swedish songs in the Grand Hall.*

To further serve those interested in the Swedish language, a group called "*Pratstund*" was formed. They meet once a week for conversations that are held in Swedish.

The Swedish calendar year, including such important festival days as *Midsommar* and *Lucia Dagen,* is celebrated at the ASI. *Midsommar* is held when the summer days are the longest, around June 21. A Maypole is raised on the museum's grounds and costumed folk dancers participate in this summer ritual. At the ASI *Midsommar* becomes a truly Swedish-American event because the customary maypole raising is combined with an old-fashioned American ice-cream social.

Dressed in traditional folk costumes, dancers participate in Midsommar festivities on the grounds of the American Swedish Institute.

Lucia Dagen is a custom celebrated on the 13th of December when the winter days are becoming short. According to the Italian legend, Lucia was a noble woman who was put to death because of her Christian faith and personal sacrifices. She was eventually canonized and recognized as a martyr for her acts in the fourth century. Saint Lucia has special significance to Sweden because she is viewed as the harbinger of light during a dark time of the year. Her name means light in latin and in early religious paintings Saint Lucia is often depicted with a ring of light above her head. This notion was adopted in Swedish tradition, in which the Lucia wears a crown of candles on her head. At the ASI the Lucia tradition is celebrated every year and includes a procession with a selected Lucia and her attendants. Customary saffron buns, called *Lussekatter* along with coffee and *glögg*—a spiced drink—are served.

This ritual is observed in most homes in Sweden, as well as throughout Swedish-America. Celebrations such as these exemplify the continuing interest in the Swedish heritage and the strength of Swedish ethnic traditions in America.

The ASI also reaches out to other parts of the state in fostering interest in the ethnic culture. Through the years several ASI affiliate groups located in Minnesota and the bordering states have been formed. These groups promote Swedish-American culture with their own programs and activities.

* *

That the ASI has continued to grow both in terms of membership and community service is a tribute to the spirit of the Swedish-American people. Their dedication to the preservation of the Swedish heritage and traditions, including the countless hours donated by selfless volunteers, has built the foundations upon which the Institute rests, and from which it can serve generations to come.

"Lucia" from the American Swedish Institute's traditional Lucia celebration, circa 1940s.

"Lucia" stands with her illuminated crown in front of the Visby Window, circa 1954.

Notes

1. A. E. Strand, *A History of the Swedish-Americans of Minnesota* (Chicago, 1910), 697.
2. C. W. G. Hyde, and Wm. Stoddard, *History of the Great Northwest and its Men of Progress* (Minneapolis, 1901), 160–161.
3. R. I. Holcombe, *Compendium of History and Biography of Minneapolis and Hennepin County, Minnesota* (Chicago, 1914), 532.
4. A. E. Strand, op. cit.; 302–303. Strand refers to a 1907 date but materials from the ASI Archives show that Turnblad was using a rotary color press as early as 1903.
5. *The Minneapolis Journal,* April 10, 1900.
6. The *Minneapolis Journal,* July 25, 1900.
7. Nils Jaenson, Swedish Vice Consul to Minneapolis in an unpublished document written in 1929, ASI Archives.
8. Hilda Benson, unpublished memoirs of the *Svenska Amerikanska Posten,* November 25, 1960.
9. *Minneapolis Tribune,* March 9, 1921.
10. *Minneapolis Sunday Tribune,* December 15, 1929.
    The Minneapolis Morning Tribune, December 15, 1929.
11. *Minneapolis Tribune,* December 15, 1929.
12. *The Minneapolis Journal,* December 10, 1929.
    Minneapolis Tribune, December 11, 1929.
    St. Paul Pioneer Press, December 11, 1929.
13. C. A. Anderson, "How the Institute Missed Out on Bequest," *American Swedish Institute Bulletin* (1961:1), 13.
14. Ibid, 13.
15. *Minneapolis Illustrated* (Minneapolis, 1889), 36.
16. Britt and Ingemar Tunander, *Kakelugnar, Spisar och Kaminer* (Västerås, 1982), 61.
17. Walfrid Engdahl, "The Last of the Institute's Carvers," *American Swedish Institute Bulletin* (1959: XIV), 3–4.
18. Nils William Olsson, "Ulrich Steiner, Institute Wood Carver is 90 Years Old," *American Swedish Institute Happenings* (1969:1), 2.
19. Ruth Sherwood, *Carving His Own Destiny; The Story of Albin Polasek,* (Chicago, 1954), 154.
20. Gertrude Gump, *The Story of Swan Johan Turnblad* (Minneapolis, 1969), 7.
21. Ibid.
22. Elmer Albinson, "The Institute's Stone Carvings," *American Swedish Institute Bulletin* (1955:X), 5, 30.
23. *The Minneapolis Morning Tribune,* November 8, 1922.
    The Minneapolis Journal, November 8, 1922.
    Svenska Amerikanska Posten, November 15, 1922.
24. Lilly E. Lorenzen, "The Institute: A Short History," *American Swedish Institute Bulletin* (1954:IX), 3.
25. Wesley Westerberg, unpublished research done while he was Director of the American Swedish Institute.
26. C. A. Anderson, op. cit., 13.
27. Nils Sahlin, "Spiced Fire," *American Swedish Institute Bulletin* (1951:VI), 21–23.
28. *The Minneapolis Morning Tribune,* July 29, 1921.
29. Marion Nelson, *Vesterheim The Norwegian American Museum* Decorah, Iowa* (Decorah:1973), 21.
30. Vera Evison, *Angles, Saxons, and Jutes* (Oxford:1981), 135.
31. Chloe Zerwick, *A Short History of Glass* (Corning:1980), 32–33.

Bibliography

Albinson, Elmer. "The Institute's Stone Carvings." *Bulletin* (of the) American Swedish Institute, Vol. X No. 1, (Summer 1955), 5.

Anderson, C. A. "How the Institute Missed Out on a Bequest." *Bulletin* (of the) American Swedish Institute, Vol. XVI No. 1 (Winter–Spring 1961). 12–15.

Bacig, Tom and Fred Thompson. *Tall Timber: A Pictorial History of Logging in the Upper Midwest.* Bloomington, MN.: Voyageur Press, 1982.

Bakke, Lorene. "A Swedish Castle in Minneapolis." American Swedish Historical Foundation Yearbook, 1964, 74–85.

Barton, H. Arnold. *Letters from the Promised Land, Swedes in America, 1840–1914.* Minneapolis: University of Minnesota Press, 1975.

Benson, Hilda. Unpublished Memoirs of the Svenska Amerikanska Posten, November 25, 1960.

Berglund, Emil. "An Intimate Account of the Founding." *Bulletin* (of the) American Swedish Institute, Vol. XV No. 1 (Winter–Spring 1960), 3–9.

Bjorling, Marie and Stanley H. Vernon. *Treasures of Swedish Art from Earliest Times to the Beginning of the Twentieth Century.* Stockholm, Sweden: Bröderna Lagerström Boktryckare, 1950.

Engdahl, Walfrid. "The Last of the Institute's Carvers." *Bulletin* (of the) American Swedish Institute, Vol. XIV No. 1 (Summer 1959), 2–4.

Evison, Vera. *Angles, Saxons, and Jutes.* Oxford, England: Oxford University Press, 1981.

Gump, Gertrude. *The Story of Swan Johan Turnblad.* Minneapolis, MN.: The American Swedish Institute, 1969.

Hammerstrom, Lawrence G. "How Much Did the Turnblad Mansion Cost?" *ASI Posten,* Vol. I No. 1 (Jan. 1982), 5, and *ASI Posten,* Vol. I No. 2 (Feb. 1982), 4–5.

Hammerstrom, Lawrence G. "The Swedish American Publishing Company Stock Holders' Law Suit Against Swan J. Turnblad." *The Swedish-American Historical Quarterly,* Jan. 1984, 39–54.

Hasselmo, Nils. "The Swedish Settlement of Minnesota," from *Swedish Minnesota—A Bicentennial Salute.* MN.: Minnesota Bicentennial Council, 1976.

Hillbrand, Percie V. *The Swedes in America.* Minneapolis, MN.: Lerner Publications Company, 1966.

Hoadly, R. Bruce. *Understanding Wood, A Guide to Wood Technology.* New York: Taunton Press, 1980.

Hokanson, Samuel. Transcribed oral history in the ASI Archives.

Holcombe, R. I. Ed. *Compendium of History and Biography of Minneapolis and Hennepin County, Minnesota.* Chicago: H. Taylor and Company, 1914.

Hyde, C. W. G. and William Stoddard. *History of the Great Northwest and Its Men of Progress.* Minneapolis: The Minneapolis Journal, 1901.

Jaenson, Nils. Unpublished document written by Swedish Vice Consul to Minneapolis in the ASI Archives, 1929.

Johnson, Carolyn E. "A Dream Fulfilled." *The American-Scandinavian Review,* Vol. LVII No. 3. (Autumn 1969), 275–282.

Johnson, Emeroy. *A Guide to Swedish Minnesota.* Minneapolis, MN.: Minnesota American Swedish Council, 1980.

Johnson, Robert E. "Swan Turnblad's 1900 Car Sensation." *Bulletin* (of the) American Swedish Institute, Vol. XII No. 1, (Summer 1957), 6–8.

Kastrup, Allan. *The Swedish Heritage in America.* Minneapolis: Swedish Council of America, 1975.

Kirn, Mary and Sherry Case Maurer. *Härute—Out Here: Swedish Immigrant Artists in Midwest America.* Rock Island, IL.: Augustana College, 1985.

Levin, Carl E. "Making Glazed Kakelugn in Sweden." *Bulletin* (of the) American Swedish Institute, Vol. XVII No. 1, (Winter 1962–63), 11–13.

Lofgren, John Z. *The American Swedish Institute Collections and Swan J. Turnblad Mansion.* St. Paul, MN.: The North Central Publishing Company, 1979.

Lofgren, John Z. *To Amerika.* Minneapolis, MN.: Reynolds Printing, 1986.

Lorenzen, Lilly E. *Of Swedish Ways.* Minneapolis, MN.: Dillon Press Inc., 1964.

Lorenzen, Lilly E. "The Institute: A Short History." *Bulletin* (of the) American Swedish Institute, Vol. IX No. 3, (Autumn 1954), 3–11.

Lyle, David. *The Book of Masonry Stoves: Rediscovering an Old Way of Warming.* Andover, Massachusetts: Brick House Publishing Co., 1984.

Minneapolis Directory, 1887–1905.

Minneapolis Sunday Tribune, Dec. 15, 1929.

Nelson, Charles W. "Model City Architecture 1870–1915 Builders Created a Rich Heritage. Can We Preserve It?" *Hennepin County History,* (Winter 1972).

Nelson, Marion. *Vesterheim, The Norwegian American Museum* Decorah, Iowa.* Decorah, Iowa 1973, 21.

Olsson, Nils William. Ed. "Ulrich Steiner, Institute Wood Carver is 90 Years Old." *American Swedish Institute Happenings,* Vol. I No. 10. (Dec. 1969), 2.

Plath, Iona. *The Decorative Arts of Sweden.* New York: Dover Publications, Inc. 1948.

Rice, John G. *They Chose Minnesota: A Survey of the State's Ethnic Groups.* Minneapolis, MN.: The Minnesota Historical Society, 1981.

Sahlin, Nils G. "Director's Report to the Members." *Bulletin* (of the) American Swedish Institute, Vol. VIII No. 2, (Summer 1953), 14–22.

Sahlin, Nils. "Spiced Fire." *Bulletin* (of the) American Swedish Institute, Vol. VI No. 3, (Autumn 1951), 21–23.

Sallnäs, Marie-Louise. "Emil Meurling and Svenska Amerikanska Posten." *The Swedish-Pioneer Historical Quarterly,* (Jan. 1981), 41–64.

Sherwood, Ruth. *Carving His Own Destiny; The Story of Albin Polasek.* Chicago: R. F. Seymour, 1954.

St. Paul Pioneer Press, Dec. 11, 1929.

Strand, A. E. *A History of the Swedish-Americans of Minnesota.* Chicago: Lewis Publishing, 1910.

Svenska Amerikanska Posten, Nov. 15, 1922.

Swanson, Evadene Burris. "The Institute's 11 Tile Stoves." *Bulletin* (of the) American Swedish Institute, Vol. XIII No. 1 (Summer 1958), 9–13.

Swanson, Mary. *The Divided Heart: Scandinavian Immigrant Artists, 1850–1915.* Minneapolis, MN.: University Gallery, University of Minnesota, 1983.

The Minneapolis Journal, Jan. 22, 1900.

The Minneapolis Journal, July 25, 1900.

The Minneapolis Journal, Aug. 27, 1901.

The Minneapolis Journal, Nov. 8, 1922.

The Minneapolis Journal, Dec. 10, 1929.

The Minneapolis Morning Tribune, Mar. 9, 1921.

The Minneapolis Morning Tribune, July 29, 1921.

The Minneapolis Morning Tribune, Nov. 8, 1922.

The Minneapolis Morning Tribune, Dec. 11, 1929.

The Minneapolis Morning Tribune, Dec. 15, 1929.

Tunander, Brit and Ingemar Tunander. *Kakelugnar, Spisar och Kaminar.* Västerås, Sweden: ICA Bokförlag, 1982.

Westerberg, Wesley. Unpublished notes on research done while he was Director of the American Swedish Institute, 1978–79.

Zerwick, Chloe. *A Short History of Glass.* Corning, New York: Corning Museum of Glass, 1980.

Index

Photo Credits